Ignatius Batory

States' Philosophy, States' Economy, And States' Finances

Ignatius Batory

States' Philosophy, States' Economy, And States' Finances

ISBN/EAN: 9783744753395

Printed in Europe, USA, Canada, Australia, Japan

Cover: Foto ©ninafisch / pixelio.de

More available books at **www.hansebooks.com**

AND

STATES' FINANCES,

Inseparable but Distinct Sciences.

———

BY

IGNATIUS BATORY,

BALTIMORE MD.

PRICE 50 CENTS.

—

BALTIMORE :
The Sun Book and Job Printing Office.
1883.

INTRODUCTORY.

For over a century, mankind has striven to obtain the knowledge, how, and through what means, it could be accomplished, that each and every individual might be enabled, through his physical or mental capacity, to obtain an easy mode of making a living.

And to the present day we have only succeeded in laying a deeper foundation for such a desire and a broader basis for its future success.

For while in the past there were but few who were exercised upon the problem, this day there are millions, whose noble aim it is to accomplish the desired object, and nearly everbody feels the need of such reform in the construction of society.

The evil has become so fully developed that those who create nothing live and enjoy the fruits of physical and mental labor, where those who create everything barely retain for themselves an almonishary existence.

The machinery through which this system has been fostered in the past was the law-making power, in the hands of the few, commonly known as the privileged classes, and supported by physical power in the shape of standing armies under the control of rigid laws, commonly called "army regulations," enacted by the same authority and controlled by the same interested parties. All laws were then enacted for the sole purpose of enriching the few and impoverishing the many. The people were taught to believe that they were subjects and had no rights but what they may receive by the deignity of the parties in power.

A system of roboth, known in the English language as *soccage service*, sometimes called fief, and sometimes called a royalty, but by whatever name you may call it, the result and object was the same, namely: to take from physical and mental labor all that could be exacted, which caused the concentration of all the material wealth in the hands of a few, to the detriment and suffering of the many.

The simple fact that the result has proven an accumulation of enormous wealth in the hands of the few has aroused the people in those times to action, and the system was gradually broken, but the same men retaining the legislative power in their hands, have gradually shaped legislation in a manner and have accomplished the same end in an indirect way, namely: through the system of *indirect taxation.*

When the framers of our form of government had undertaken to free this continent from the English, they were instigated by the same course, namely : "the attempt by the men in *power to levy extraordinary taxes.*" From this attempt and from this course sprung the Declaration of American Independence, and the consequent Republican form of government. *A simple and cheap government. The object of the framers of our government was a cheap government and happy people.*

The aim of the people at that age was already directed to establish a form of government that might enable each and every individual to gain *an easy mode of making a living*, through his physical and mental capacity.

The desire and aim of all good men of our present generation is the same. But how to accomplish it is the great question.

Some propose to obtain this desirable result through the establishment of supreme authority in communes.

Others have advocated socialism, something of the character and nature of our trades unions and Knights of Labor, but they have failed to prove practicable, and the problem is not solved yet to this day.

The framers of our form of government have upon this question mainly relied upon the principle of self-government for its accomplishment, of which they gave proof by asserting in the outstart that their object was to secure safety to life, liberty and the *pursuits of happiness*, securing to the people the safety of life and the liberty of action that they, *the people, may secure to themselves and posterity the pursuits of happiness. Idem est—an easy mode of making a living.* From the above facts it would be convincing to every candid mind, that it is the duty of every one in society, who esteems the worth and moral of the above precepts or teachings, as left to us as an inheritance by our ancestors, *to co-operate for their accomplishment.*

We propose to give you advice, through which advice you will be enabled to possess yourself of the key (to unlock the mysterious chalice out of which society has and does yet drink so bitterly) that will enable you to solve the mystery.

We do not intend to bring proof from other sources for the correctness of our conceived knowledge, for we claim to be original in our conceived ideas, consequently we have no predecessors to cite from upon this all-absorbing social science. But we kindly ask your deliberate consideration, satisfied that we are able to convince you on all reasonable questions involved, satisfactorily, and to gain your convincement.

For you will perceive from the foregoing, that from time to time, from generation to generation, the few have managed to live upon the expense and ruin of the many—the people.

You will perceive also that the means employed to accomplish such end was the legislative power. For the maxim, that all that is good and all that is evil in society emanates from legislation, is true.

You will also perceive that society did only move in opposition when wealth and power became concentrated and all-powerful by corrupting public men, to influence legislation. We are in such a condition again.

You will also perceive that the people failed to remove the evil from the inability to find a practical remedy.

You will also perceive that the fathers and framers of our institutions and of our government mainly relied upon the right of franchise, as secured by the constitution, for the gradual accomplishment of the desired object expressed in the sentence, " pursuit of happiness."

You cannot help perceiving also that we have failed till this day to secure the avowed object, namely : to obtain an easy mode of making a living. And the failure results from the same causes and through the same channels, namely : the connivance and corruption of the men in office ; and to-day we are exhausted through means of *extra-ordinary indirect taxation*, which brings *poverty, corruption and submission to our land of freemen.*

For in place of the older doctrine, that you have no rights but what the privileged classes deign to grant you, they have invented the rule of (party nominations) by themselves. They call this Democratic or Republican rule, but the object is *office, bribes, peculation, rings, contracts, jobs, trusts,* and often outright *robbery, causing enormous outlays that prevent the attainment of happiness through our pursuits or calling.*

PREFACE.

1

Take all the wisdom your mind can grasp, the balance will take care of itself, till some one else will perceive it.

2

Logical conclusions are at times the most ungrateful productions. They are by others distorted, perverted, misconstructed, ridiculed, thwarted and at times even slandered to serve an opposite interest. Therefore each individual must judge for himself!

3

The mind of men is like fire, it must have fuel to continue to burn. That fuel is independent thought.

4

If you have attained on any subject a conviction, stand by it, reassever it under all circumstances, till you find out that you were mistaken, and when that happens, be man enough, honest enough to state it on proper occasions.

5

State's Economy, in a free country like ours, must mean increased production and increased consumption. Multiplication of the demand for labor and an increased capacity of consumption.

It must mean the employment of all available labor in the community or nation, increasing the material prosperity of the people. And not the prosperity of the government, corporations or individuals.

6

To govern a nation is a science "hidden but sure," and when properly comprehended and applied, the test proves itself in the prosperity of the majority of the people.

7

Nothing is more destructive to the material happiness of a nation than the ill-chosen representatives to the legislative body.

8

Free Press, when neither partisan, sectarian, nor bribed, is the noblest achievement of civilization.

9

To be rich and sympathize with the poor is one thing, but to be poor itself is another thing.

10

Create circumstances through the agency of legislation "that will compel the circulating medium to seek income and profit" through the channels of trade, commerce and agriculture and shipping *direct*. And hard times will disappear like the mist, on the appearance of the Sun.

11

The best prevention of insanity and suicides is centered in such economic laws that will have a tendency to increase the chances and values of mental and physical labor.

12

The material prosperity of the laboring people does not depend as much on the form of government, as on the character and aims of the financial and fiscal laws that prevail in the nation.

13

There is an *inseparable mutuality of interest* between the laboring man and the employers of labor. The brewers are interested in the ample earnings of the shoe-shop hands, to enable them to consume their product.

The shoe manufacturer is interested in the ample earnings of the laboring men that work in the breweries, as it does enable them to buy shoes.

The tailors are also interested in the ample earnings of the shoemakers and the brewery hands, that they may be enabled to buy clothing.

So are all other callings, be they physical or mental occupations. They are all mutually dependent on the prosperity of each other.

There is no exception. The medical men, the minister of the gospel, the scientist, the merchant, the manufacturer, the holder of real estate, the whole of the human brotherhood and sisterhood, the married and the single, are all mutually interested in the prosperity of mankind. To obtain this desirable end look to legislation.

14

Such a condition of society could be best accomplished by following the legislative methods as propounded by me in the following document, *written and published in the year 1868.*

4

[Written for the People's Weekly, *January* 18th, 1868.]

DISCUSSION OF THE FINANCIAL QUESTIONS OF THE DAY.

BY IGNATIUS BATORY,

Vice-President of the Labor Reform Party of the Third Legislative District.

No. I.

MESSRS. EDITORS:

The great question of the times is the financial; all other questions—industry, commerce, agriculture, revenue, taxation, reconstruction, etc.—are secondary, and in fact dependent upon the solution of the first named. This being my conviction, I take the liberty of asking the privilege of using your valuable columns for the treatment of the subject of finances from a standpoint (quite novel) of my own.

For more than twenty years have I tacitly been observing the movements of public men as leaders and moulders of the destinies of nations; in consequence of which observations, I became convinced of two facts: First, that acknowledged leaders are not always wise or honest. Second, that the above-mentioned characteristics are rarely united.

From hence follows the partisan spirit in individuals, and consequent incapacity (for doing good) of whole bodies of men, whom they may lead.

To solve the financial questions of our country, safely and judiciously, requires wisdom and honesty combined. Wisdom, to give satisfaction to both debtors and creditors. Honesty, to do justice to all, the individual citizen who creates all wealth, and the individual citizen who possesses and enjoys wealth without infringing upon the natural and lawful rights of either, and at the same time secure safety and stability to our form of government for all time coming.

It is not the purpose of the writer to criticise our public men for the theories they have advanced, in relation to this all-absorbing question. It is sufficient to enumerate the measures proposed and advocated by some of them and give our objections.

The proposed measures resolve themselves in the following : Contraction and Expansion.

First, contraction, as advocated by the Secretary of the Treasury on one hand, and by Honorable R. J. Walker on the other, (in spite of the latter's assertion against contraction). Contraction as proposed by the Secretary of the Treasury, coupled with funding of debt, retention of the national banking system, and resumption of specie payments, to strengthen the government credit, as avowed by the Secretary, will increase the coin interest paying liability of the government, and at the same time give an undue advantage to those who own the government obligations in bonds and currency. At the same time it will have a tendency to reduce the price of labor to such an extent as to enable capital of this country to compete with European labor (this seems to be the hidden object of the Secretary of the Treasury), at the expense of the misery that inevitably would befall the industrial and agricultural classes of the nation. For to admit, for a moment, that capital in America, being secure of six per cent. interest in gold for a time coming, as a minimum rate of interest, will be able to compete with capital in Europe, that is worth but three per cent. is preposterous, and can be only accomplished through the agency of cheapening labor, instead of cheapening capital; exacting at the same time an income or revenue sufficient to pay the interest and expenses of the government, from the industry and agriculture of the people.

As to the proposition advanced by the Hon. R. J. Walker, to raise a loan of $1,000,000,000, in gold at six per cent., in some foreign country, to resume specie payment and to retain the national banking system, serious objections present themselves. First: borrowing $1,000,000,000 in coin, if it could be had, would in itself be a calamity to the laboring and agricultural classes of the country, for in a few years the interest upon the same ($60,000,000 per annum) and the present banking laws retained, would be sufficient to absorb the whole amount, leaving the government in no better condition than she is at present and the people oppressed with a burden that no republican government can guarantee, and undoubtedly would bring about the very calamity of repudiation, which all honorable men desire to avoid. Second : it is inconsistent for the interest of capital to trust itself to the borrower (*idem est*—people) when the borrower exercises the judicial power, in the form of legislation. It is therefore dangerous for a free people to create an interest that will, under certain circumstances, favor a change of political system, for the safety of its material wealth. Such interest, if centered at home, may be oppressive to the people, but cannot wrench from the people the right of legislation and consequent power of self-preservation. But let this nation assume a responsibility of such magnitude to citizens of other nations, with the express condition that such obligation shall be litigable in some foreign country, it will create an interest abroad that at some future day will claim a right to control our legislation, when such legislation shall address itself to finances. Such claims will in such case surely be supported by the identical interest at home, and the writer has no doubt that it would become a source of corruption in our legislative halls, unparalleled in the annals of time. Moreover, it would cause our people to become indirectly the supporters of foreign powers; for, under the present financial laws, no matter how heavily our people may be taxed, the wealth of the country has no undue outflow.

As to the resumption of specie payment, for the restoration of confidence, this assumption seems to be in conflict with the well-established fact that that a nation which is capable of producing the most over and above what she consumes is the safest to trust to.

As to the second proposition, to expand the United States currency to a sum commensurate to the wants of exchange of commodities, for the retirement of national currency, and the paying off of our indebtedness in currency or coin, as per contract made when negotiated, in principle we do agree, but as to its practicability, under present circumstances and laws, we object. For, to put such a system in operation without precautionary laws, would enhance the price of all commodities to such an extent that the more currency we would issue the more would be needed as an equivalent fo the purpose of exchange ; and such a system would leave the country in an unsettled condition, for no one would know the actual value of things from day to day. What we need is a judicious and stable system, so as to fortify the rights of capital and the right of those who possess no capital but their industrial capacity, and to secure safety and unimpaired enjoyment of production to industry as well as to capital, upon principles of equality and protection—in unison and accord with our form of government. Capital is in its nature inclined monarchically, for it needs when concentrated a strong power for its protection, (a concentrated government) ; consequently arises the necessity in a democratic republican nation, of decentralizing capital in order to secure the safety and interest of the people and government.

" Decentralization of capital," then, must be the political standpoint of democratic-republican finances, verifying the asserted principles of equality and independence to people and government.

The next question to be considered is, how decentralization of capital shall be accomplished, without infringing upon the rights of the individual possessing and holding of property on one hand, and relieving the industrial classes from the grasping grip of capital on the other hand. Upon which subject we propose to treat in our next.

[Written for the People's Weekly, *January 25th*, 1868.]

CONTINUATION OF THE DISCUSSION OF THE FINANCIAL QUESTION OF THE DAY.

BY IGNATIUS BATORY,

Vice-President of the Labor Reform Party of the Third Legislative District.

No. 2.

MESSRS. EDITORS :

In our first letter we have endeavored to prove that the policy of contraction, funding and national banking system, or the policy of borrowing money from Europeans, upon a gold basis, will have a tendency to concentrate capital in the hands of the few, (as before), and create an interest against the people's rights, and will endanger, ultimately, the form of government which we all profess to cherish and to appreciate so much.

On the other hand, that the policy of expansion of the legal tender currency, under the present financial system and laws would, in itself, be ruinous ; for the distrust it would engender in all branches of industry, the consequence of which would be financial chaos and confusion, the end of which no one can foresee. Asserting at the same time that the policy of decentralizing capital must be the standard measure of democratic republican finances.

Having thus taken this position in favor of decentralizing capital, in a judicious and lawful manner, we venture the following as the best mode known to us for its accomplishment, based upon these grounds :

That capital being the medium of exchange, for all things known to civilization as property, acquires, through this propensity, a superiority of influence over the natural capacities of men, (physical and mental). *And when strengthened in this position, by privileges acquired through the agencies of the law-making powers, not properly comprehended when enacted, or enacted in a spirit of partiality, it becomes the master of both mental and physical capacity, and retains to itself the power of control and aggrandizement.*

The propensity as a general medium of exchange is a blessing to society, for it stimulates production. The privileges acquired through legislation is a *curse* of which society should be relieved ; and, as we understand the case, it is centered mainly in the right of suing in the courts for collection of loans voluntarily made. Let the nation declare that every business transaction is to be considered cash on its face ; let the nation abolish all the usury laws, make capital a free commodity, give the owner the right of charging interest to his satisfaction, but abolish the privilege of collection through the agency of a court ; let it be understood, that he who trusts assumes the responsibility of the collection.

· Let the nation next restrict capital from absorbing and monopolizing the soil, in the shape of real estate, public lands, &c., so that this natural gift to men shall be unobstructed ; then capital will be forced back to the channels for which it was created.   Industry, commerce and agriculture will find in capital their *best friend, instead of its master;* for capital, once stripped of its extraordinary privileges, will be brought in a position equal with the mental and physical capacity of men—all resting upon their true usefulness ; capital will lose its power of control over the industry, agriculture, commerce and government ; depending as it would upon mental and physical labor direct for its profitable employment, it would become its assistant, instead of its ruler ; mental and physical labor will each regulate itself, every individual would be enabled to enjoy the fruits of his *time* and *capacity, unimpaired.*

Capital, finding itself dependent upon the industry, commerce and agriculture of the land, will expand our productive capacity to an extent never before known Our shipping will revive, to carry our surplus products to every nook and corner of the globe ; for cheap money is the grand lever of industry, and money *(once stripped of the privilege of lawful usury, fostered by an insane credit system, supported by courts, paid for by those who are to be stripped of all they can earn by hard toil,)* will be cheap.   The masses will become the government, the government will be stronger, safer, and more free than ever before.

Let the nation therefore pass, all over the United States, enactments : First—That the usury laws in all the States being abolished, all business transactions hereafter being considered cash upon their face, that creditors assume the responsibility for the collection of debts.

Second—That all courts for the collection of debts, voluntarily entered into, or contracted, shall be abolished.

Third—That the soil being a natural gift to men, shall not be monopolized by individuals to a larger extent than so much per capita, *through acquisition hereafter.*

Fourth—Repeal all laws relating to our present mode of taxation, and enact laws upon the principle of direct taxation, (*for, to decentralize capital, it is necessary that those who own the wealth of the country shall be taxed for its support, and those who own nothing but their productive capacity should not be taxed.*) Such laws would enable the poor toiling and industrial classes to accumulate property and become taxpayers. No citizen should be required to support the government materially further than the amount of material wealth he actually possesses at the time so taxed, for although moral and mental support in time of peace, and *physical support in time of war*, is due from every one of its citizens, *material support cannot judiciously be exacted but from those who possess the material wealth in the government.*

Fifth—That all laws now in force that grant privileges exclusively to individuals or corporations prejudicial to the material interest of the majority of the people, are in conflict with the natural rights of men, and ought to be repealed, from time to time ; and no similar laws should be hereafter enacted.

Capital once deprived of its undue powers, of controlling our government, will cease to be a corrupting element ; *physical, moral and mental capacity will become the standard value of men;* and the capacity of our industry and agriculture will be the true standard value of our *credit* and currency, as a nation; for a nation that is capable of producing the most, over and above what she consumes, is the safest to trust to ; coin will inevitably flow to its threshold. Coin will become a commodity of exchange only, without strength to control the natural powers of men.

Capital, forced to the channels of industry, agriculture and commerce, (for which it was created), for its profitable employment, will become the best friend of the people and government, and not be any longer its controlling master. It will assume a dependent position ; will employ itself in all branches of the national industry, agriculture, commerce and shipping ; the last named it will revive to an extent never before known in the history of any nation ; for it is the high rate of interest it is able to secure upon land, that prevents it from being employed upon the seas, and gives an undue advantage to other nations, in this particular branch of industry and commerce.

Not through the contraction of the circulating medium, then, but through the contraction of the rate of interest on capital, depends the revival of production and consumption, (industry and commerce), and the *re-establishment of our credit as a nation.*

Where interest upon capital is excessive, there living becomes expensive, and industry, commerce and agriculture, not finding the productive capacity of the people sufficiently remunerative, as to leave a surplus means for the consumption of the products of the alternate branches, becomes stagnant and oppressed.

Money becomes scarce, not for its scarcity, but for the fact that when interest is at 12 per cent. but half the amount of capital is required for the absorption of the surplus means of the productive capacity of the nation, as when capital is 6 per cent.

Let us assume, for the purpose of illustration, that the legislation we advocate would have a tendency to place capital in a position that it would be willing to employ itself at a rate of 2 per cent., *when safe investment could be made*. Then it would take six times the amount of circulating medium to carry home the surplus production of the nation, as at the rate of 12 per cent.—consequently our present paper currency, if not expanded, would not be sufficient to absorb the surplus production, and coin would follow its trail to gain the balance.

An individual who, at present, is in possession of $500,000, and manages to gain a ten per cent. income, say of $50,000, would then earn but

2

$10,000; the balance of $40,000 would remain with those who produce all gains, through their mental and physical exertions. The industrial, commercial and laboring classes would be enabled to retain a sufficient share of the fruits of their time and labor, to enrich themselves, become truly free and independent, and enable them to become supporters of the government materially ; the government will increase its tax-paying population, become stronger, safer and freer.

The nation will be enabled to reduce its interest-paying obligations to one-fifth, part of the interest as paid at present, instead of repudiation. She will also be enabled to conduct the government upon a less outlay as at present, in proportion as the rate of living is to become cheaper.

The currency at present being $700,000,000, taking in consideration the amount of business done through the agency of the banks by drafts, checks, &c., it cannot be less than twice as much, say $1,400,000,000 ; add the coin in the country, $500,000,000, and we have a total circulating medium of $1,900,000,000. Abolish the courts to collect by and you abolish the present banking system with them, then the government, by withdrawing the present national currency, will be enabled to issue $1,400,000,000 of currency without causing inflation.

The government currency being circulated through the agency of the treasury department, will not be used as a medium, to exhaust the resources. of the people, through the agency of discounts, as done at present, multiplying interest upon interest, till a total absorption of all the wealth of the country is inevitably to take place in the hands of the few. For, through the medium of raising the prices of all necessaries of life, the middle classes are reduced to poverty. Capital absorbing their means, creating want and demoralization, the consequences of which enables capital to use those wretches (small politicians) as a lever against the interests of the laboring classes.

The grasp of concentrated capital once severed from the people's pocket, by abolishing all laws, granting special privileges, through which privileges capital is at present enabled of controlling by indirect means, mental and physical capacity of men. It will then assist the development of the use of modern appliances, as steam, machinery, railroads, electricity, &c., for the furthering of our productive capacity, and will increase our industry and commerce, instead as at present, being but a speculator upon the same, by means of discounts.

It is the duty of American democratic republican statesmen, not only to secure to their fellow citizens the enjoyment of the right of life, liberty and property against direct attack, but also from indirect encroachment.

Capital, as the laws stand at present, encroaches upon the resources of industry, agriculture and commerce, to an extent that the acquirement of property becomes difficult, and in many instances, unattainable. In consequence of which liberty, and even life's worth, seems dubious.

Our present statesmen seem to consider this all-important question from a European standpoint, namely : Capital, Government and People ; where there ought to be but two parties—Capital and Nation ; (the last government and people.)

Capital is compact selfishness ; it unites with government in a mutual bond, to secure interest to the first and power to the second.

In Europe a nation never borrows money ; it is always the government and capital that compose the parties to the contract. The people are only considered in their productive capacity, as so many sheep to be shorn, just as a great wool producer does to raise a loan upon his next crop of wool. The moneyed man exacts the lowest possible price as a reward for his advance payment. So does capital exact the best terms—loaning upon bonds at the lowest figures and securing the highest rate of interest, so that by the volume of interest it (capital) may be able to measure the standard of value, of its received bonds, after the close of the negotiation.

The people are never consulted (in Europe) in the matter, consequently there a nation never borrows. For a nation is composed of *people* and *government.*

The principles of finance are in Europe well understood ; the government and capital unites there, for a mutual advantage. Capital upholds the government by furnishing the ready means for sustaining standing armies, a machinery, through which the very laws enacted by the government, to create its own authority (without consulting the people), are enforced on one hand, and the laws to secure unimpaired revenue to, and safety of capital on the other.

Here lies the secret, why money is worth in Europe but 3 per cent., and in the United States 6 per cent., the latter being the wealthiest and the most productive ; but does not possess the same guarantee in the form of standing armies and absolute power.

Our present government is yet republican in form, but does not possess, beyond the ballot, the essence of a democratic government, which is the people's rights, interests and influence in the government—which rights, interests and influence can be secured to them only through the securement of *material* independence.

[Written by Ignatius Batory, for the People's Weekly of Baltimore, February 8th, 1868.]

THE WORKINGMEN'S PARTY AND ITS MISSION.

It is not well understood by our fellow-citizens for what purpose this new party is organizing. Like all new things, it is subjected to doubt and distrust. On the other hand its principles not being (as a general thing) fully developed, it stands in exactly the same position to the two parties relatively, as do the two contending parties (democrats and republicans) stand in relation to each other namely : "struggling for the mastery." We can, therefore, expect no favor from either. For we assert that neither of the above-named parties have a fixed or well defined platform of principles to stand upon, comprehensive enough to embrace the interest and well-being of the *whole American people*. They are both struggling for a mastery of position *only*—office and its emoluments.

We beg leave to inform our doubting and mistrusting fellow-citizens that, although our principles are as yet not fully developed, they are sufficiently so to enable us to claim for them a *superiority* in comprehensiveness and of general usefulness as well; being calculated for the benefit of the whole American people.

For the essence of the principles of the Republican Party in power at present, is, *universal or manhood suffrage.* Ostensibly for the purpose of securing safety to the form of government, but in reality for the strengthening of their (Republican Party) chances in the electoral college for the next presidential election. To attain this last mentioned advantage securely, they are compelled to bring their battle-cry—universal and manhood suffrage—in conflict with their action, by disfranchising a large number of citizens—voters heretofore—which is neither universal nor manhood suffrage.

Such policy is neither in *principle* nor in *fact* comprehensive, nor for the well-being of society — being wanting in MORALITY, JUSTICE AND EQUITY.

The essence of the principles avowed by the conservative or Democratic Party, is, "the Constitution as it is." This as a battle-cry sounds well to the ears of the American people. So do we want the preservation of the American Constitution. But the Democratic Party has for the last fifteen years, and especially the last few years, given sufficient proof of its inability to keep within the limitations of the Constitution, and stands, in this respect, upon the same record with the

Republican Party, although for different purposes. The consequence of it is political demoralization ; that there are not two leading Democrats or Republicans in this country who view the Constitution with the same comprehension.

Both of these parties are deficient in capacity of judging CORRECTLY, MORALLY, or COMPREHENSIVELY. They stand before the people as plaintiffs and defendants, each accusing the other, for the purpose of lightening the burden of political sins that rests upon their names respectively, and from which the people have been and are yet suffering so intensely.

This proves their incapacity for public or general good. They are not representatives of the people, the entire people, for they have neglected their material welfare, and consequently can never become comprehensive, for they are *partisans* and not *patriots*.

In each of the States, we may as well assert in each of the Congressional districts, of the Union these partisans have an interpretation of *their own*, for that venerable (and vulnerable) instrument, the Constitution.

This is certainly not a comprehensive enough principle, through which the general good of the nation can be secured.

As to the all-absorbing interest of the people, the very substance of life, liberty and happiness— the *financial question*—these parties stand upon the indentical ground or platform, namely : "Let it alone, do nothing ;" for they each desire in the next election, the support of the workingmen and of capital as well. Object :—The MASTERY OF POSITION ONLY (office and emoluments.)

Such a policy, such a platform, such a no-principle, is certainly neither comprehensive, nor for the general good of the nation.

OURS IS A NEW PARTY, JUST EMERGING FROM THE PEOPLE. IN OUR BODY THERE ARE NO OUTGROWN OR OUTWORN POLITICIANS. WE HAVE NO KNOWLEDGE OF POLITICAL STRATEGY OR POLITICAL TACTICS. WE HAVE NO PIPES TO LAY, NO MINES TO DIG, NO LIES TO CONCOCT, NO AMBIGUOUS LANGUAGE TO STUDY, NO POLITICAL HYPOCRISY TO FEINT, NO FALSEHOODS TO UTTER. We stand upon the TRUTH and nothing but HONEST TRUTH, as it becomes MEN, Democrats and Republicans—as citizens of a free and common country.

What we profess, you can rely upon. We may be mistaken, or we may be wrong, but never will any one be deceived by our party. For the people cannot deceive themselves, their wives, their innocent children, suffering as they do. Let them but listen to our professions. "GOOD TO ALL AND EVIL TO NONE" is OUR BATTLE-CRY.

Free government with us signifies free people. A people that suffers for the want of peace, harmony and happiness, or the want of an *easy mode of making an honorable living*, *is not* free and consequently have a no more free government than a monarchy has.

The object of this party is to be true to its mission. We feel it is the duty of a party, if it be Democratic or Republican, to represent the best interest of the whole people. This is what neither of the other parties do. To retrieve our lost ground of freedom, to re-establish actual, in place of present nominal freedom, and to improve upon the original, by preventing in future, (through the enactment of laws, impartial in their nature,) the centralization of an influence over the government. To create a financial system that will enable each individual to make an honorable and easy living, and to retain the surplus of all he earns. To destroy the artificial channels, created through the assistance of legislation of half a century, erroneously conceived or partially enacted, and through which channels all the wealth of the country flows to the few ; and to enact laws in their stead that will have a tendency to cause the wealth of the country to flow to the many and make them truly independent. To destroy the habit of idolatry of MEN, and to teach idolation of principles, of laws, and of the Constitution; of morality, of impartiality and of self-sacrifice for the public good.

To abolish the present system of indirect taxation, as being destructive to the material independence of the people, and to establish a system of direct taxation, upon the principle that each citizen shall be taxed in proportion to his material wealth.

To prevent crime and pauperism, by furnishing the means of making an honest living.

To prevent debauchery and prostitution, by furnishing the means of support, to enable the young to contract early marriages.

To restore the moral comprehension of the people, by entrusting none to high or responsible offices but men who will conscientiously regard the obligation of the Constitution and the laws.

To ennoble and to elevate the character of the young, by enabling them to earn a support and protection for their aged or infirm parents.

To make this nation the most happy, the most virtuous, the most noble, the most independent, and actually free.

The mission of our party is to verify the aspirations of the framers of this our government, to make men free, independent and happy. In fine it is the mission of this party to fulfill the obligations imposed on us (as men) by nature, through the laws of nature, from which all rights take their origin and authority.

GOOD TO ALL AND EVIL TO NONE"—is the motto of the Workingmen's party.

• [Written February 22nd, 1868, by Ignatius Batory.]

THE WORKINGMEN'S PARTY—WHO ARE TO BE CONSIDERED WORKINGMEN?

———————————— .

When the great majority of the nation are forced to seek relief from the oppressive circumstances they are brought under through the means of organizing a political party, that will represent their interests fully, and chose to style it "THE WORKINGMEN'S PARTY," it becomes of import to ascertain and to know, who of the citizens of our country are indicated in the name "workingmen," and whose interests is, by the nature of their occupation in society, identical and inseparable from the movement.

In Europe, where society is headed by Emperors, Kings, Queens, Princes, Dukes, Lords, Counts, Barons, and others of nobility and rank "enjoying extraordinary prerogatives and privileges," it follows that men (human nature being imitative) crave for superiority, privileges and position, to assimilate themselves to rank. "And as rank cannot retain its position and influence safely, except by keeping others as inferiors, at the same time, could not maintain its pretensions against a united sentiment of the people,—it (rank) is creating a divided interest (apparently) and aspirations."

Rank fosters a belief in superiority of men over men—from which they deduce the divine right of the minority to rule the majority—and creates inferior ranks and classes, based not upon privileges, for they are all subjects, but upon the following: 1. Wealth; 2. Learning; 3. Profession; 4. Merchants; 5. Manufacturers; 6. Artisans; 7. Clerks; 8. Boss Mechanics, (small employers); 9. Mechanics; 10. Farmers; 11. Servants; 12. Workingmen. This fostered and inculcated belief of imaginary superiority between men and men, constitutes the weakness of the majority (the people), and enables the minority to maintain its prerogatives and privileges, and to retain the whole mass, the learned, the professions, the merchants, the manufacturer, &c., as subjects—ALTHOUGH THEIR INTERESTS ARE IDENTICAL!

This very notion of superiority seems to have crept into our society, and has retarded the development and perfection of our free institutions—thus the principles of justice, equality and happiness, as enunciated by the framers of our form of government, have been entirely lost sight of, and there is to-day no liberty beyond the ballot-box.

Each branch in society is assuming a position of superiority over their fellow men, loosening themselves from the natural tie, that binds the interest to the whole ; neglecting to fulfill their duty to the weaker portion of their fellow men, still pretending to be sensible, honest, virtuous, and God-fearing men !

This being our condition, it behooves us to attempt to prove the identity of interest of all those whose occupation is agriculture, industry, commerce, mental or physical labor, in our country.

Let us examine for a moment how our interests are bound together. All interest in society is, in its nature, founded upon material well being. The emperor or king would not be willing to retain authority, if it would give ease and happiness to his subjects, and entail poverty and trouble to himself. No person would be willing to serve as President, as Senator or member of Congress, if it would cause him trouble and loss of a corresponding amount of wealth as it at present benefits him. It is then from a material standpoint that we have to view our common interest.

There can be no misconception in regard to our chosen name, that of " The Workingmen's Party," containing as it does laborers, servants, mechanics, small employers and artisans. Of the others we will take up the merchants, the manufacturers and the agriculturists.

The merchants divide in two interests, the productive and exporting and consumptive and importing capacity of the nation. To increase the productive or exporting capacity of the nation, we must force capital into the channels of industry at the lowest possible rate of interest. Capital will increase our production, and the low rate of interest our export. To raise the consumptive or importing capacity, we must relieve the people of the oppressive taxation and unjust legislation that ,enables capital to exact its present high rate of interest, exhausting the earnings of the people, preventing them from being consumers to any great extent.

The manufacturer has an identical interest with both the above classified merchants. He needs cheap capital and a large consumption.

The agriculturist needs cheap transportation, cheap goods, cheap money, and liberal consumption. If we force capital into industry at a low rate of interest, the farmer will be able to purchase his groceries, merchandise and implements at a low figure, and by relieving the people and himself of the unjust mode of taxation, he will find the people able consumers.

Professional men and clerks both need cheap living, low taxes, and the people's capacity to employ their respective branches, theirs being undoubtedly mental labor, being the natural twin brother of physical labor.

As to the learned professions, we cannot enlighten them, for if they have not sense enough to know their identical interest with labor, they certainly do not belong to the learned professions.

We aver that nearly every individual in our country is a co-workingman in a national sense, each doing his best for his advancement singly, and for the nation jointly. Socially NO EVIL CAN BE DONE WITHOUT AFFECTING US ALL. The laws that prejudice the interest of one member, prejudices the interest of all.

The merchant is but a clerk of his employer—"THE PEOPLE"—either for procurement of the necessaries from other countries, or for the disbursement or exportation of our own surplus products. The manufacturer is not less a workingman of the nation than is a common laborer, each working physically or mentally for self—and jointly for the nation. The farmer ranks, in Europe, below the mechanic; admitting him in this country an equal position, but certainly he should not think himself better than a workingman, for work is his existence.

In fine, the interest of all is identical, the laws that oppress one oppress all. There are few exceptions only and they are those possessing an interest disconnected from industry, commerce and agriculture, and standing upon the merit of capital or office, the latter being the most dangerous to the best interests of the people—it being based upon aristocratic family relationship, or upon *subserviency* to *capital* or party interest.

Let, then, all good men unite for a joint effort to DISLODGE CAPITAL, *and the unprincipled, subservient politicians from the political power that enables them to attain their selfish ends, to the injury of the majority, to an extent that no prerogative or privilege in Europe has ever been able to accomplish to such perfection.*

LET US (THE WORKINGMEN'S PARTY) UNSADDLE THESE CRUEL RIDERS, FOR THEY FORCE THEIR SPURS INTO OUR FLESH !

[Written March 21st, 1868, by Ignatius Batory.]

WHAT WE HEAR, WHAT WE READ AND WHAT WE FEEL.

We hear, we read, of the noble progress made by the workingmen's party everywhere. We are gladdened, we are pleased, we are hopeful, we feel elated—but what of all that? What does it compare with the grand aim of our movement!—the success of which is destined to give a Fatherland of our own to the toiling millions—a home full of plenty, of peace, of happiness, of innocence, of love, of attachment, of manhood, of independence and contentedness.

YES! OUR SOUL HAS PENETRATED THE YET HIDDEN FUTURE, and it has lit a spark there, that has laid bare to our mind's eye, *the future that is sure to come*, when every one will be happy and free!

Down, then, with party predilections! For the people must be made happy and free!

We implore you, workingmen, to come forward and trust to the workingmen's party. We possess hearts to feel, minds to judge, souls to penetrate, to convince, to search for the good of us and you all.

Let those who choose, sneer, laugh or jeer, we will win, for the good of all. And those who now sneer, laugh or jeer at us, and those who even degrade themselves by slandering, falsifying, traducing or betraying us—will, to their own shame, be compelled to enjoy the benefits of our success in common with us.

. For under all circumstances the workingmen's party will remain true to their mission, to bring good to all and evil to none.

Our object is a legitimate one. It is to awaken the people to the danger that threatens them and their posterity, from the political demoralization and incapacity of the public men of the day. *It is to show them the future as we see it, for good or evil.* Then it will entail upon them to choose between their present condition—homeless, needy, quarrel-ridden, tax-ridden, bank-ridden, without means, without peace, without happiness, despoiled of innocence, of love, of attachment, deprived of manhood, of independence, and content; or the future, as we comprehend it—a fatherland of their own, a home full of plenty, of peace, of happiness, of innocence, love and attachment, a consciousness of manhood, independence and contentedness.

We must compel dishonest politicians to work for a living, by taking the offices from them, and enact laws that will cause all those who do not work to starve, and will enable all that do work to make a living, instead of as at present that those who work starve, and those who do not work live to enjoy.

It is the duty of every workingman, then, to come forward and attach himself to the movement, ally his feelings to those who candidly profess and urge him to self-deliverance, from the gnawing jaws of the political hydra.

[Written by Ignatius Batory.]

DESIDERATUM VIRGINÆ EST POTENCIA.

The thought, the wish, the cravings and aspirations in the individual, constitute and are the powerful agencies that plant the germ in the seed of thought in men, from which springs civilization and human achievements.

It is the individual who thinks first, wishes first, craves first, and aspires first for the obtainment or accomplishment of a certain desirable object; he being convinced of the practicability, beneficent and equitable character of the desired object. He follows it up with an inspired zeal that nature plants at times in men. He thinks, feels, and he reiterates his thoughts and feelings to his fellow men, for his conclusions are worthless to him without the assent, approval and assistance of his fellow men.

Science, Religion and States' philosophy assimilate themselves to the new thought, and humanity is benefited by it.

DEMAND AND SUPPLY.

DEMAND AND SUPPLY IS THE SUBTERFUGE OF
IGNORANT STATESMEN AND THEIR FOLLOWERS.

Whenever the ill-conceived policy of our States'
economy and States' finances culminates in commercial panic, our all-wise statesmen, at the head
of our administration, who manage the peoples'
affairs, as a rule, express themselves, that demand
and supply regulates these things, charging over
production, high living, extravagance and so forth,
as the foundation of the evil.

The truth is, our people don't produce enough,
don't consume enough, don't spend enough, which
I will right here endeavor to prove to you. Suppose our people were prosperous, by being enabled
to find constant employment utilizing their physical and mental labor, they would consume more,
produce more and spend more otherwise, than
they are enabled to do at present.

Our nation contains at least ten million families
or households of six persons each. This is statisti-
cally ascertained.

These ten million households by being enabled
through the agency of prosperous times, would

use the trifling amount of one pound of meat additional per diem.

This would increase the demand for meat of thirty-six hundred million pounds per annum. Equal at ten cents per pound, to five hundred million dollars.

It would require three million and six hundred thousand cattle, each weighing one thousand pounds when dressed, or thirty-six million head of sheep, one hundred pounds each.

If each family would have the means to buy an additional one pint of milk per diem, the consumption of milk would increase thirty million quarts per week, not counting Sundays, or equal to three hundred and seventy-five million gallons estimated at ten cents per gallon, does represent the sum of thirty-seven and one half million dollars.

Each family by using *one* pound of butter in addition to the present consumption per *week*, calculating it at twenty cents per pound, represents the sum of one hundred million dollars.

By adding one pound of lard to each family per week, we gain at eight cents per pound, forty million dollars per annum.

If each family had the means of buying two barrels of flour per annum in addition, this would consume twenty million barrels, representing, at five dollars per barrel, one hundred million dollars, requiring one hundred million bushels of wheat, or more than our present surplus.

Assuming prosperity in every American household, each one of them would use the trifling amount of fifty cents per week on fruits, vegetables and green relishes in addition to their present consumption.

This amounts to two hundred and fifty million dollars per annum.

Reader, I will stop here, as I do not desire to enter into the infinite of possibilities, to burden your mind or waste your time. Be it sufficient that I have here enumerated only six leading articles of an indispensible nature, the aggregated amount of which is eight hundred and eighty-seven and one-half millions dollars. A sum sufficient to pay the wages of nearly two million men, at ten dollars per week for one year. The production of the wealth here stated would inure entirely to the agricultural industry of the country, would benefit the means of transportation and trade and commerce.

Assuming further that by creating prosperity through just legislative means, we would also enable our people to spend annually each on shoes additionally two dollars. This would increase our industry and commerce one hundred and twenty millions. One dollar on hats, sixty millions, two

3

shirts each at seventy-five cents, ninety millions; clothing three dollars per annum, one hundred and eighty millions; underwear one dollar, sixty millions; furniture five dollars a family, fifty millions; carpets and oil cloths, three dollars, thirty millions; stoves and cooking utensils five dollars, fifty millions; crockery, glassware and cutlery, three dollars, thirty millions; pictures and ornaments, two dollars, twenty millions; paper-hanging and drapery two dollars, twenty millions; painting and renovating the houses, five dollars, fifty millions; making in all seven hundred and sixty millions, equal to the wages of one million five hundred and twenty thousand men, at ten dollars per week for one year, or in all, equal to the wages of three millions and twenty-seven thousand men at ten dollars per week for one year. This being a larger number of men than this country ever had out of employment.

Reader, these are no imaginary conceptions; these are facts based on reality. Labor is idle waiting to *create, earn* and *consume;* mental and physical labor is craving for opportunities to create, earn and enjoy the fruits of labor and the blessings of nature! But they are prevented by ill conceived economic and financial legislation.

The people are prevented from creating annually the immense amount of *eighteen hundred mil-*

lions dollars worth of property by being kept in idleness, through the invisible hand of combined wealth and power.

It is our duty to *increase* the *prosperity* of *every American household*, by decentralization of wealth and decentralization of power. This can be accomplished through judicious legislation. *By preventing the circulating medium "Money" from making an income outside of trade, commerce, industry, agriculture or shipping.*

[Written 1875, by Ignatius Batory.]

STATES' PHILOSOPHY, STATES' ECONOMY AND FINANCES.

.

———————

States' philosophy, States' economy and finances, are three inseparable sciences ; the failure in one causes the failure in all.

Our present financial system is apparently a success, but will actually prove a failure, as it lacks the States' philosophical and economical virtues.

Our present financial system is grounded upon the conception of governmental credit. Just as a merchant strengthens his credit by paying promptly, principal and interest, although his resources are daily impaired to a larger degree, and his ability to pay in the future becomes less.

States' philosophy teaches us that in a government like ours, the ability to pay should not be calculated beyond a reasonable portion of the annual surplus of the earnings of the people, and not from the *positive or actual possessions already acquired* by a portion of our people, for such a policy impoverishes the tax-paying portion of the people, the very foundation of national credit

For the stability of the credit of any nation depends entirely upon the material prosperity of the people and not upon the disposition of the government to exact income, and when the people have the legislative power to estop their government from impoverishing them, governmental guarantees become feeble, consequently. The present financial policy of our government is fallacious and unstable.

If we view our financial policy from a State's economical point of view, we find that it is calculated to encourage our people to become usurers upon the resources of their fellow-citizens, avoiding all risks of industry, commerce, agriculture or shipping, which causes millions of our laboring men to be idle, and consequently diminishes our resources of production, reduces the surplus earnings and endangers the material prosperity of our people. No philosophy, no policy that is not calculated to advance the chances of constant employment to mental and physical labor is sound, and all calculations and promises that are not based upon production are fallacious and futile. States' economy bewares us of unemployed labor.

We must legislate in a manner to force the circulating medium into the channels of trade, industry, commerce, agriculture and shipping, for which channels it was created. Legislators must endeavor to create circumstances through the agency of well matured laws, equitable in their nature, that will have a tendency to force the circulating medium in a position that would compel it to seek income or profit through the channels of trade, industry, agriculture, commerce and shipping direct, and not as at present. It obtains profit and income in an indirect manner, without risk or exertion on the part of its possessors. And the very authority that was created for the protection of the interest of the *weak* and *innocent* (the people) acting as agent to convey the earnings and possessions of the many to the few (the usurers and the office holders.)

The philosophy of our present financial system is the cheapening of labor, by increasing the purchasing power of the circulating medium, centralizing wealth and power where it ought to be decentralization of capital and decentralization of power.

[Written by Ignatius Batory, September 6th, 1892.]
[The article below was published in the *Baltimore Sun*.]

THE LABOR SITUATION.

Mr. Ignatius Batory writes to *The Sun* as follows: A conflict of material interest is steadily gnawing at the peace and stability of society and endangers our free institutions. Wm. H. Seward once stated in relation to slavery and freedom that there is an irrepressible conflict going on, and that either the one or the other must perish. The consequences and the result of the above conceived philosophy are to-day known to all of us. There is an irrepressible conflict steadily going on to-day between the many and the few in regard to the division of the *surplus earnings* of the human race.

Some believe in the philosophy of a divine or providential, and consequently destinal, arrangement, that the humble, the ignorant, the credulous and the poor must look to the hereafter for relief and alleviation. Some again believe that there should be organized or established by law a grand social union, national in its conception and paternal in its aim—all to join in a common effort to produce and consume the products of physical and mental labor—*idem est*, socialism—to accomplish which they propose to regulate the hours of labor, the price to be paid for such labor, and also the division of the surplus profits of labor. . Others again advocate a total absorption of all the wealth by the government through the respective communities, and hold it in trust for the use and benefit of all the people; compel each individual to do a share of production for the common fund of stock—*idem est*, communism.

There are also a great number of men who are not willing to accept the theories of either of the parties mentioned above, namely, of those who believe in the poor man's destiny in a reward hereafter, or of those who advocate the philosophy of socialism, nor of those who advocate communism, and having nothing to propose themselves, make use of a stratagem that demand and supply does regulate this question. They don't seem to know that the people are restless upon the very question of demand and supply. Now, will such subterfuge, such humbug avert the irrepressible conflict?

Let Democratic and Republican statesmen ponder. The people are restless. One ounce of prevention is better than a pound of cure. Demagogism among the politicians and demagogism among the people must be met to avert danger.

The remedy lies in a strict adherence to the spirit and letter of our constitution. The material prosperity of the confiding people must be made the corner-stone of our free institutions and the aim of our statesmen. The present conceptions of States' philosophy, States' economy and finances must be abandoned and brought back to the sub-serviency of the material welfare of the people, and not as at present, being the means of absorbing all the surplus gains of physical and mental labor by the few.

The interest of the business men, manufacturers and farmers are identical with the laboring men.

It is the politicians and the legislative traffickers that destroy people's chances of prosperity and disturb the equanimity of our institutions.

Honesty, coupled with ability, must be invited to re-enter the public service; to apply its capacity to the discovery of the methods that will lead to the solution of the problem that naturally is attached to our free institutions—institutions that in their wake carry the necessity to make the citizen *materially independent*.

The philosophy of non-interference by the few and decentralization of power must be steadily kept before the eye of the mind of our legislators. No undue advantage ought to be permitted to exist against man and man. Men of mind and

honor must be enlisted into the service of the
people such as will serve the people, and not a
party nor of a combination of men for selfish ends.
In our days the name of the people is abused by
their representatives in the legislative halls, who
cunningly pass laws to enable the few to absorb
the annual surplus of earnings of the race. To
maintain our peace and free institutions we must
seek the remedy. *It can best be found through the
agencies of economic and financial legislation.*

[Written by Ignatius Batory, May 18th, 1888.]

SOME ECONOMIC QUESTIONS.

In a letter to *The Sun* on current questions of the day, Mr. Ignatius Batory writes as follows:

Usury or *interest* on the *circulating medium* and *indirect taxation are the two monsters* that have *enslaved the many to the few.* It is but the urbaric system of a half a century ago renewed in an indirect manner; changed from direct oppression into a hidden but at present legalized robbery. If I had the power I would have laws passed that would prevent the circulating medium from obtaining income or profits except through the channels of trade, industry, commerce, agriculture and shipping. Such action would increase our production and commerce, at the same time multiply the demand for labor, and greatly increase consumption of the products of the nation. Prevention is better, and will be less costly to society than an involuntary cure. State philosophy dictates the decentralization of power, and through its agency the decentralization of wealth, in this our free republican form of government. This duty is devolved upon the lawmaking powers in Congress and in the respective States, but must be accomplished in harmony with the *ex post facto* feature of our constitutions. Wherever there are iniquities obtained or created through the errors or cunning of past legislative bodies, they ought to be looked after and repealed. Wherever there is a system that has grown up in our nation that has a tendency to enable the few to obtain income or profits from the many without returning an equivalent in mental or physical production, there the legislators ought to step in and apply the sovereign authority by enacting preventives. To prevent the possible destruction of these our free institutions, and the possible ruin of all the accumulated wealth, art and civilization, including the maxim of *meum* and *tuum*, it becomes imperative that the States' economy and States' financial system should be brought in harmony with the States' philosophical conceptions of the framers of this our form of government.

[Written by Ignatius Batory.]

As to the interest of workingmen in the policy of high tariff or free trade, there is none in his favor in either instance. It is always against him. The annual production of $7,000,000,000 distributes but one-fifth for labor or earnings of every description; the balance is absorbed by an invisible hand through the agency of the circulating medium, the medium of exchange, which is a system created by law, but is deceptive and against the interest of those who create. It is immaterial what amount of wages he earns per week, the cost of living will always grow in proportion. The four-fifths of his creation he will not obtain as long as the present mode of legislation is in the hands of men whose interest is on the opposite side.

Our American States' philosophy is all right, but our States' economy and States' financial systems are all wrong. Those who create all wealth are to be dupes until they know how to legislate. The leaders who create divisions amongst the labor organizations are treacherous to the best interest of the poor, ignorant and credulous workingman; unity of sentiment and unity of action is imperative. Knaves and traitors alone will keep the people divided. Outside of politics there is but shame and oppression.

[Written by Ignatius Batory.]

COMMUNISM, SOCIALISM AND SINGLE-TAX.

Suppose you give the man the land, can he till enough of it by himself at the present day to obtain a comfortable living for himself and family, and at the same time contribute to the cost of protecting society?

Can he utilize labor or time profitably enough to maintain himself and family from cutting timber, or from free fishing? At best in either instance he will but ooze out a life, miserably.

The intellect of the human race has been developed "immensely" in this century. Education has become general and the tastes and cravings for comfort have steadily been growing in the people proportionately to that development.

Industry to-day creates things that our ancestors never dreamt of, and consequently had no craving for such.

The annual income of the laboring people of the present day is manifold larger than it was a century ago, but the necessities and cravings of to-day being developed in the ratio of our industrial development, causes want and consequent suffering.

The remedy is not and never will become effective either through communism nor through the modern socialism or single-taxism.

It can be accomplished through the agencies that underly the philosophy of our institutions, if properly conceived and acted upon. Non-interference by the few against the earnings of physical and mental labor of the people and decentralization of capital (money), are the guiding stars that will ultimately lead this nation to the much desired object of the prosperity of every American household. Each citizen will be independent in his own orbit. The people will be protected from *indirect injury* as well as from *direct attack.*

The credulous, the ignorant, the confiding, the debased will find protection through impartial legislation? Personal liberty will go hand in hand with material prosperity and independence.

Material prosperity in every American household is and must be *per se* the outcome of our free institutions. Self governmen when properly comprehended by the majority of the people will accomplish it. Be assured it is not an impossibility.

EVOLUTION, OR MORE CLEARLY CONCEIVABLE AND BETTER DEFINED AND UNDERSTOOD AMALGAMATION.

It is nature's tendency to amalgamate "the human race," not only physically but also spiritually and mentally.

The mind of the human family is more susceptible to amalgamation and mingling than the physical body, as the mind forces its influence imperceptibly and invisibly upon the mind of fellowmen.. Therefore, there is no resistance or repugnance to hinder the immutable.

The thing that must come, surely will come.

The human family is destined to be acknowledged by all mortals at some future day, as one brotherhood and sisterhood.

The question arises, shall it be a common family? Fed from a public kitchen, clothed from a public warehouse, sheltered in public lodgings, entertained in public parlors and theatres, all to be owned by the State or the States.

On the other hand, shall all production be co-operative or mutual? Or shall it be individuality, as at present, each individual striving for himself, and indirectly for the community at large, moving in his own orbit, obtaining all the benefits from his physical and mental powers that nature endowed him or her with, subject "only" to the rules, regulations and laws of the community, each individual obtaining protection for himself and guaranteeing protection to all others, maintaining *"individuality" and independence* under the restriction of "non-interference," either through direct or indirect methods, with the *interest of others.*

If preventives are enacted by the law-making power, it will cause *decentralization of wealth, "at present in the hands of the few,"* just as certain as the present methods do, in an indirect manner, cause centralization of wealth and consequently centralization of power. For the centralization of wealth means also centralization of power, and is a sure destructive element of the *freedom, happiness and independence* of the citizens. "It is the duty of the State to guard against such a possibility." Therefore to obtain prosperity, we must protect the personal interest of the citizen against *indirect injury* and prejudice; we must create a financial system that will have a tendency to enhance the value of physical and mental labor, by *multiplying the demand for the same. State's economy is not to save, to diminish, to contract, or to hoard, but to spend, to increase, to expand and to disburse.*

The economy of the citizen to advance his personal interest should not be confounded with the economy of the State. The first does well to hold on to all he can "honorably." The last, *the State, does best by disbursing all.*

It is the "prerogative," the exclusive right of the State and community, to control the disbursement of the surplus earnings of the people so it may cause rotation in the channels of trade, industry, agriculture, commerce and shipping, from *whence the prosperity of the people emanates.*

The equitable division of the surplus earnings of the nation, therefore, is the great problem of the day.

This question has at different times forced itself to the attention of our law-makers, but as a rule it was dismissed as a matter that will adjust itself through demand and supply,

At present our economic system enables the few by and through the assistance of a false "theory of finances" to absorb the major part of the production of the many—"the nation."

The legislative and administrative branches of the government, "*States and National,*" indirectly are favoring such outcome, and at times even the courts have been made available to further this *concentrated and gradually more and more grasping power.*

What is to be done? Where is the remedy?

[Written by Ignatius Batory.]

Not willing to claim superiority over any other proposed remedy, we still feel that it is our duty to ourselves and to the inceptions of truth, justice, equity and impartiality, that underlies our proposition, to claim that our States' philosophy, States' economy and States' finances as presented by us in the year 1868, and republished in this pamphlet, possesses the advantage of being harmonious with our present constitutions and laws, not being in any way in conflict with the *ex post facto* feature of our constitution.

Securing to each citizen protection under the laws remedying the future (and not the past), preventing in an indirect manner, through legislation, the interference by the rich, the cunning and the scheming politicians, with the mental and physical productive capacities of men, in the *future*, causing hereafter each individual to be independent in himself, working hours to suit his purpose and interest best, obtaining remuneration in accordance with his skill, ability and perseverance. Enhancing labor by the circumstance of preventing either capital or land to obtain an undue advantage through legislation.

Poverty of the people arises from the circumstance that the surplus profits from productive mental and physical labor are absorbed by the few favored ones by the aid of legislation.

States' philosophy, States' economy and finances are three distinct sciences. Still they are inseparable in their nature, for the failure of one causes the failure of all three.

[Written by Ignatius Batory.]

States' philosophy, States' economy and finances, the three inseparable sciences, the failure in one the failure in all.

It is not comprehensible to the ordinary mind of man that it is easier to level society down than to elevate it, for it requires comprehensive capacity and skill to elevate, where want of comprehension and consequent failure will accomplish the lowering down of the material, moral and comprehensive capacity of society, and destroy its noblest aspirations.

Our present generation is absolutely baffled in her career through the machinations of her leaders, in whose minds there is no science but one, and that is politics as a trade, with its adjuncts of bribery, ballot-box stuffing, repeating, perjury, intimidation and ultimate fleecing of the betrayed.

Under such circumstances prosperity and happiness becomes an impossibility.

The foundation of State's economy rests upon the employment of labor, not as much by the State directly as through the circumstances created through legislation.

[Written by Ignatius Batory, May 17th, 1885.]

TRUE AND FALSE CONVICTIONS.

Men generally assume and state so, that this or that is their conviction, where in fact there is probably but one in a thousand who has ever formed an independent conviction. To form a conviction we must exercise our vision, our hearing and our best mental faculties: vision to examine by where necessary, hearing to obtain information *pro* and *con*, and mind to mature by, to enable us to obtain a conviction. Convictions assumed from other sources are but believes, and believes are but structures without a foundation.

[Written by Ignatius Batory, August 11th, 1879.]

We must guard against a landed aristocracy; for if we ever succeed to force the circulating medium into the channels of trade, by such legislation that will prevent it hereafter from obtaining income "through the medium of interest on credit investments," they will certainly instantly seek to monopolize the renting power of real estates, and through such agency, obtain a controlling foothold over our commerce, industry, and trade in general ; and reinstate themselves in a position towards society "that will enable them to obtain the surplus production (the increase of annual wealth) of mental and physical labor, causing the steady centralization of wealth in the hands of a few non-producers, as at present. For such is the aim of all monopolies!

[Written by Ignatius Batory, January 1st, 1888.]

Discussion of the economic questions that force themselves upon our present generation, and threaten to disturb the equanimity of our people, if not the destruction of our, the most equitable, the most judicious, the most beneficial and most free form of government.

From observations and convictions, in relation to the question of States' Economy, Finances, and States' Philosophy, as relating to the present labor agitation and unrest, as conceived by me, through a period of more than one-half of a century.

It is not my purpose to *combat* or *approve* "theories or teachings" of other worthy men and citizens, who honestly teach what they believe to be *truth*, therefore, ought not to be blamed for the fallibility of men.

I am not in conflict with the George land theory, for while it is not a remedy to accomplish the

deliverance of the people, it is true in its inceptions, that the earth belongs to the whole of the
human race, as a gift by the Creator. And the
proposed method of taxation is legal and within
the powers of States and National government,
capable of dispossessing its present holders.

The iniquities that rest upon the shoulders of
the many, in favor of the few, at present in this
country, are *manifold*, and like a very weighty
bridge on pillars, the removal of one pillar increases
the pressure on the others. And in a true sense
there is no relief whatever.

The proposition to raise all taxes from land
would not prevent the few from absorbing the
surplus earnings or profits of the nation, derived
from physical and mental labor. Such absorption
is done through the agencies of interest on the
circulating medium, bonds, stocks, mortgages,
ground rents, discounts, unlimited railroad charges
for freight and passengers, and manifold combinations and tariffs to enhance articles and commodities that enter the daily consumption of the people.

All these evils can be prevented by abolishing
the right to sue in court, or to collect by process and
assistance of the courts. The credit system and
the right to sue for collection of voluntary-given
credits on one hand, and indirect taxation on the
other, *are the two monsters that have enslaved the
many to the few.*

It is but the urbaric system of half a century ago renewed in an indirect manner. Changed from direct oppression into a hidden robbery.

Prevention is better and will be less costly to society than an involuntary cure. States' Philosophy dictates the decentralization of power, and through its agency the decentralization of wealth in this our free republican form of government.

This duty is devolved upon the law-making powers in Congress and in the respective States.

Wherever there are iniquities obtained or created through the errors or cunning of past legislative bodies, they ought to be looked after and repealed. Wherever there is a system that has grown up in our nation, that has a tendency to enable the few to obtain income or profits from the many, without returning an equivalent in mental or physical labor, there the legislators ought to step in and apply the sovereign authority of legislative pruning.

To prevent the possible destruction of these, our free institutions, and the possible ruin of all the accumulated wealth, art and civilization, including the maxim of *meum* and *tuum*, it is imperative that the States' economy and States' financial system should be brought in harmony with the States' philosophical conceptions of the framers of our form of government.

In observationis legenda natura non est criminis.

[Written by Ignatius Batory, April 13th, 1886.]

IS THERE ANY WONDER THAT THERE IS A PERIODICAL GROAN OF DISTRESS?

The present system of laws, as relating to the financial and State economical management by the States and the United States administrations, are calculated to *insure* a large part of the production that emanates from the physical and mental labors of the people annually, to a source that never produces anything, commonly known as "income on investments." Those holding and possessing these investments have no interest in the increase or multiplication of production, as their share of the aggregate profits in hard times, or surplus profits in good times, of the people's making, is securely brought to them periodically, by and through the medium of the established authorities, of the States or of the United States.

The custom house, the internal revenue department, and the tax gatherers, are the mediums of the constituted authorities, through which the annual surplus is taken to the few from the many. This is what creates the rich and the poor. This much is the direct cause of society's endangered position of this day.

To this is allied the system that legalizes the use of the circulating medium (money) on usury, such as mortgages, ground rents, loans, etc.

On the other hand, nearly all these investments are exempt of taxation, which causes the burden of the States, respectively, and the United States, in general, to be upon the shoulders of those who are least able to stand it.

Is there any wonder that there is a periodical groan of distress?

Where is the remedy? Is it in labor unions? No! Is it in co-operative shops? No! Is it in strikes? No! Is it in anti-prison labor system? No! Is it in arbitration? No! Is it in civil service reform? No! Is it in compulsory copartnership? No! Is it in eight hour laws? No! Can socialism remedy it? No? Can communism remedy it? No! Partnerships between employers and employes? No! Where, then, is the remedy? It is in honest, intelligent, judicious, impartial and *constitutional* legislation.

Upon all financial and States' economical questions, the vote of labor, if intelligently managed, can accomplish it by sending to Congress men who are by occupation, mental training and sympathy in harmony with the material interest of those who labor, physically or mentally.

Written by Ignatius Batory.]

TARIFF.

1.

Tariff is naturally a tax on the article that some one needs, consequently is paid by the consumer. It follows that a high tariff is a high tax and a lower tariff is a lower tax upon those who need the respective articles. It does incidentally protect some industry proportionately as the amount of tax collected. But the benefit accrues to but a few, and stands as special legislation in favor of a few against the many. It is class legislation, not in harmony with free government. Direct taxation, in proportton to wealth possessed, is the method that can and will assist to secure the prosperity of the many—"the poor."

2.

If a chapter is not clear to your mind, read it over and over again, till you perceive its wisdom or folly.

3.

The writer has patience with the fallibility and ignorance of men. Therefore be charitable.

4.

The ablest young men in the land can't make a successful honest stand, simply because the invisible hand of governmental legislation is against the possibility of their success.

Dislodge the usurer, the Wall-street gambler, the trusts and the courts to collect by, and your chances of making a living in commerce, industry and agriculture will be restored like magic. And the independence of the man will be joined by prosperity of the man.

5.

The interest of England is to prevent the masses in India from becoming prosperous, educated or independent. The people of India are subjects to the crown of England, and can but be kept there through poverty, ignorance and submissiveness. About four dollars per capita is her circulation. A nation of two hundred and eighty million people to be kept down by a handful of Englishmen, naturally must be governed by a State philosophy different from ours.

6.

There is an indivisibility between the human being's mental and physical necessities and productions. The more the one produces, the more the other craves for ; the more the other devises, the more the one produces.

It is marvelous, but it is in keeping with the wisdom and forethought of our invisible and our incomprehensible Maker.

It seems room for all and plenty for all was the object and intent of our Maker.

7.

Liberty, independence and rights, secured and guaranteed by Bill of Rights or Constitutions, are but expressions or assertions that bring no good, except the people or those entrusted by them with the leadership, give force and character to the spirit and letter of such. (Constitution or Bill of Rights.) Every citizen must be alive to the issue.

8.

The best remedy for the people to relieve themselves of the oppressive present, and attain a better future, is always this: Change the men and party that represent the present and the past into a party for a better future.

If your country is in a condition that you can't earn an honest livelihood through diligent labor or any other honest calling, then your laws and lawmakers are at fault. And it is your duty to change them, irrespective of by what party name they may be known.

9.

Grasping for power, for power gives them money, and money keeps them in power, the two go together ; just so goes poverty and subjugation.

Why not decentralize capital and power and prevent poverty and subjugation of the people ?

10.

The human being is like the flying star that illuminates the surrounding heavens in its flight and disappears, but differs in consequences. For while the one leaves no trace behind, the other inspires his fellow-beings to thought, action and results.

11.

The great curse that weighs upon society so heavily centres in the conception of the word "interest." Interest on investments, instead of profits from undertakings. The first is obtained out of society's possessions already acquired without risk or employment of physical or mental labor. Where to obtain profits the second is bound to take risks by employing labor, which causes them to be incidentally benefactors to society at large.

12.

The value of money or capital (circulating medium or medium of exchange) increases or diminishes proportionately, as it is enabled to invest itself in interest-bearing securities. And commerce, industry, agriculture, &c., are prejudiced or benefited accordingly.

Legislation should aim to cause capital to seek profits in the diverse channels of industry, commerce and agriculture, for which it naturally was created, which can but be accomplished by diminishing its chances of profitable usury.

Monopolies to obtain exorbitant profits in their undertakings must have a surplus of labor to enrich themselves.

Competition in the labor market is indispensable to their aims. *Protected by high tariffs*, they are secured against outside competition, and the employment of thousands of hands in the undertaking, enables them to obtain labor at their own price. A reduction of twenty-five cents per day increases their treasury by thousands of dollars daily.

[Written by Ignatius Batory.]

The silver question, simple in itself, has been for years a favorite theme for designing bankers, usurers and servile legislators. The amount of "nonsense" that was spoken about it, "apparently with fervor," in the House of Congress, in the United States Senate, and in the columns of the daily and monthly (scientific) press, would more than gird the globe. It was all done to confound the people; those interested know that in muddy water is good fishing. As to trade, industry, commerce, agriculture or shipping, it is immaterial if our currency is silver, paper or gold, as its stable value depends on the credit and guarantee of the government. To obviate this confounded question in the future, let the government recoin all gold and silver coins upon a basis of eighty cents to the dollar, guaranteeing the one-fifth, and make it redeemable at all time in full in bullion, silver or gold at market value at the option of the holder. This would also prevent the exportation or hoarding of coins.

Gold and silver must be kept a commodity, and the legal tender "money" should be prevented from becoming a commodity, by lessening its intrinsic value. Therefore, a portion of it should be based upon the credit of the government.

The idea or conception that our dollar must be worth a hundred cents in the metal is treacherous and misleading. For it enables hoarding, exporting and "manipulating," creating artificial scarcity of money and consequent depreciation of the possessions of the people, including labor, and is in favor of those who possess the ready cash, and live on interest or usury.

[Written by Ignatius Batory, Baltimore, November, 1889.]

THE PAN AMERICAN CONGRESS.

Presumably this Congress was invited by our American Statesmen, for the purpose of gaining the good will and wishes of these small American States, through the agencies of showing them our mechanical, industrial, commercial and agricultural progress. As also our military possibilities in case of war with foreign nations.

It is well to gain the reputation and respect of these weak nationalities and influence their future policy and action, and endeavor to gain their commercial favors. But as interest rules men, it also rules nations, we may be outbid at some future day by others.

I suggest a method that will hold good for all time coming, and will make their and our commerce inseparable, namely: Let the Pan-American Congress unite upon the following plan for a uniform circulating medium (money):

Let the American Nation and each of the respective States represented in the congress, agree to recoin all the gold and silver coins in circulation at present in their respective countries, and issue

instead, a new coin upon the basis of four-fifths
($\frac{4}{5}$) value, namely : eighty cents of the respective
metals, to represent a legal dollar, each government promising to redeem at all times its legal
coins in bullion, say in not less than twenty dollars. That is to say, although the dollar contains
but eighty cents of the metal, the respective
governments will, in exchange, give one hundred
cents worth of the metal, in bullion, optional with
the respective governments to pay either in silver
or gold bullion. Each nation may retain its
national emblem or imprint on the coins as at
present in vogue. Such coin of uniform value,
would soon be accepted as a medium of exchange
for commodities between these American nations
and stimulate commercial intercourse. It would
place the smallest of these nations upon an equality
basis with our own nation, and consequently could
not but be pleasing to all. Indirectly, it will prevent the hoarding of the circulating medium by
speculators and keep it for what it is created, as a
medium of exchange. Industry, trade, commerce
and shipping will profit by it, for it will not be
exported to foreign lands on account of its less
intrinsic value than the bullion that is obtainable
at pleasure.

The great problem of society in the near future
is, anyhow, to prevent the circulating medium from

making any profit or income outside of trade, commerce, industry, agriculture or shipping, for the retention of the circulating medium in the above enumerated channels will surely multiply the demand for labor and create general prosperity.

[Written by Ignatius Batory.]

The war for the elimination "of the unavoidable mistake of the fathers of the republic" from our political system (slavery) has entailed upon our nation an immense cost in lives, destruction of property and public debt. No honest citizen will question the sacred duty of the nation to liquidate the debt in full. Our form of government is a three-fold—legislative, administrative and judiciary. There has of late years arisen a question of great material importance to the people of this country, in regard to the power of Congress to authorize the issuance of legal tender paper money. This question has happily been decided by the highest court of the land in favor of such power possessed in Congress.

The Democratic platform has repudiated that decision, although the Democratic majority in Congress has not seen fit to pass a bill to verify their assumption, that the legal tender power is not justifiable. The Republican party for the last twenty years in power "after the war" has done all and everything to saddle the people with burdens in public obligations and monopolies, the consequences of which are causing our present materially distressed condition, growing out of the centralization of wealth and power in the hands of the few.

The advent of the Democratic party ascending to power entails upon it the responsibilty of solving the *labor question.* It involves questions of States' philosophy, States' economy and States' finances from a new point of view, assimilative with the requirements and object of our free institutions. It also involves the regulations of the functions of the circulating medium, taxation, and the source from where it may be drawn. Chartered privileges, (that grant prerogatives *indirectly*) and the observation of constitutional limitations, and other kindred questions.

The first step to solve the labor question, or in other words, to improve the condition and to secure material prosperity to those who either mentally or physically labor and create all that we *society* enjoy, is to enlist into the service of the administration of affairs of the nation, men who are able, honest, generous, patriotic and disinterested ; men who have proven reliable and worthy in private life ; men who will apply all their qualifications for the perfection of our free institutions ; men who will guard the interest of those who through circumstances created by poverty, were forced into a condition of credulity and dependence ; men who will apply their whole being for the solution of the problem of decentralizing power and wealth in an equitable and lawful manner; men who will not look upon the office as a creation for their special purpose, commonly known as politicians, *who make politics a livelihood*, who after they obtain office feel no other responsibility.

An honest Congress and administration to begin with is the inevitable necessity for the improvement of the material condition of American households. Such can never be accomplished through the men who wielded power in the last fifteen years, be they Republican or Democratic politicians. They are but schemers for self-aggrandizement and unable to comprehend or grasp the complicated questions that slumber like a volcano beneath our social fabric, which when stimulated by want, superinduced by the suspension of commercial and industrial activity, may burst forth at a time when least expected, and cause destruction to most of what civilization and peace in our midst has created for half a century. Prevention is surer than cure. Forethought is forearmed. Let us have a truly honest administration of public affairs. Material prosperity in the household, is the corner-stone of true independence and moral civilization. Politicians of the past are not the men who can accomplish much good. Honesty and truthfulness are rarely in them. Let us obey

the laws as they are, call in the public debt, pay
it in legal tenders. Relieve the people of the
interest. It will force the capitalists into enterprises that will benefit mental and physical labor.
This is the first step to solve the labor problem.

It is a well-known fact that the Supreme Court of the United States have decided that Congress, acting for the people, has the power to issue legal tender paper money for all purposes. The democratic party leaders, while dissenting from that decision, and having seen fit to express their dissent in the platform of 1884, have, nevertheless, since their advent to power, not ventured either to approve nor to challenge that decision.

The right of the people to issue legal tender paper money is, at the present juncture of our commercial and industrial condition, of immense consequence.

The issuance of legal tender circulating medium either by the *respective States* or by the United States, becomes at this juncture of our industrial condition an unavoidable necessity. *It is the lever that alone can quicken the motion of trade, commerce, industry and shipping* and enhance agriculture.

It is an admitted fact that there is a disparaging condition between those who create the wealth and those who possess the wealth of the nation.

The controversy is not as to the existing facts, but as to the sources of the evil, and the means of remedy.

To inflict injury and inequality upon the majority of the people, the cunning few have used the legislative power, in violation of the fundamental principles of the constitution. To restore equity to our people we must return to the first principles, as enunciated by the fathers of the Constitution.

It is the interest of the wealthy to arrogate powers beyond the constitutional limit, *under plausible, but false pretenses.* On the other hand, the interest of the poor is to cling to the strict construction of the limited powers as provided by the Constitution. As the first leads to the concentration of wealth, the second is .a preventive and is calculated to shield the people from aggression by the designing few.

The non-adherence till now by both parties, to the decision of the United States Supreme Court in relation to the issue of legal tender, and ignoring its possibilities in a commercial and prosperity point of view, proves their shameful indifference to the people's interest and welfare.

There are at present outstanding nearly fourteen hundred millions of United States bonds that are subject to redemption with this legal tender. Why not pay them off, save the annual interest, and increase commercial enterprises to the extent of the amount of the circulating medium to be issued.

It would enhance the value of labor proportionately as the circulating medium in the hands of the present bond holders would increase. It would enable laboring men to obtain abundant employment.

It is a part of statesmanship to create demand for labor "through legislation" in an indirect way. The guarantee of the national government on the bonds being considered sufficient. Why not also on legal tender notes?

Only lunatics will deny the *fact* that the commerce of the country solely upon a gold basis is an impossibility, except upon the destruction of freedom and the substitution of servitude of the people.

[Written by Ignatius Batory.]

AN AMERICAN FINANCIAL SYSTEM MUST BE HARMONIOUS, JUDICIOUS AND CONSEQUENTIAL.

———:———

Harmonious with the philosophy and intent of our American Constitution as relating to the material welfare and personal rights of each and every one of our citizens.

Judicious by stimulating trade, commerce, industry and agriculture without permitting some favored ones to sponge upon the economic branches of the nation through the agencies of usury, special privileges, combinations and trusts, and so forth.

Consequential by preventing the circulating medium by indirect means from obtaining income or profit through any source whatever, excepting through the employment of labor direct:

Without the above essentials no financial arrangement will work satisfactorily.

[Written by Ignatius Batory, February 22d, 1880.]

1910 AND 1920.

All railroads will be condemned and paid for by the respective States; no more public securities will be emitted, and all that may be outstanding will be subject to taxation; no more mortgages or ground rents will be recorded; no more debts will be collected through the agencies of courts, as all business transactions will be considered cash on their face (in law). A maximum will be set for the ownership of real estate by each citizen.

The national administration will issue all the silver and gold coins, but no paper money. The States will charter State banks and decide upon its guarantee, if coin or real estate. Import duties will be collected upon the principle that all articles that the country can produce a sufficiency of will be *lightly* protected, and all articles that the nation cannot create a sufficiency of will be admitted free. All high protective tariffs and all subsidizes will be forever banished.

Legislation will incessantly aim at forcing the circulating medium into the channels of trade, commerce and industry by preventing its employment in usurious or chartered speculations. Taxes will be collected in a direct manner, taxing each citizen in proportion to his possessions. All charters that grant monopolies will be repealed or condemned and paid out of existence, as the right of suing in court for the collection of debts will be abolished, the usury laws will disappear, credit will be based on honesty instead, as at present, based on property. Bribery, ballot-box stuffing or false count and false voting will be punished like arson or rape. The intelligence of the people will make it impossible for rough and dishonest men to obtain public positions of trust. The meaning of the words, democrats and republicans, will be well understood as being identical, the people will rally upon measures and not names.

[Written by Ignatius Batory.]

THE FRUIT IS RIPENING ; IT WILL SOON FALL INTO THE LAP OF SOCIETY !

For half a century in vain did I try to enlighten fellow men in relation to the iniquitous system of finances and its uses. In vain did I make the effort to prove to fellow-men the cause of his poverty on one hand and the concentration of immense wealth on the other hand. In vain did I try to convince fellow-men that our form of government does fully warrant his prosperity.

In vain did I try to make fellow-men see the roots that cause his poverty and debasement. But they could not see ! In vain did I speak the words of plain reason ; the seed fell in untilled ground. But the evil will soon remedy itself ! For necessity is a great teacher

[Written by Ignatius Batory.]

THE END.

I love humanity not for its being human, but for its being sublimely created, by a sublime power and for sublime purposes, that centres in generosity and love that will ultimately culminate in the happiness of all! For such is the intention of our Maker as exemplified by the powers of thought, feeling and conscience implanted in mortals.

INDEX.

www.ingramcontent.com/pod-product-compliance
Lightning Source LLC
Chambersburg PA
CBHW032358280326
41935CB00008B/621